Pebble™ Plus

Animal Homes

Beavers and Their Lodges

by Martha E. H. Rustad

Consulting Editor: Gail Saunders-Smith, PhD
Consultant: William John Ripple, Professor
Oregon State University
Corvallis, Oregon

Mankato, Minnesota

Pebble Plus is published by Capstone Press
151 Good Counsel Drive, P.O. Box 669, Mankato, Minnesota 56002
www.capstonepress.com

1 2 3 4 5 6 09 08 07 06 05 04

Library of Congress Cataloging-in-Publication Data
Rustad, Martha E. H. (Martha Elizabeth Hillman), 1975–
     Beavers and their lodges / by Martha E. H. Rustad.
     p. cm.—(Pebble plus. Animal homes)
     Includes bibliographical references (p. 23) and index.
     ISBN 0-7368-2582-7 (hardcover)
     1. Beavers—Habitations—Juvenile literature. [1. Beavers—Habitations.]
I. Title. II. Animal homes (Mankato, Minn.)
QL737.R632 R87 2005
599.37—dc22   2003024902

Summary: Simple text and photographs illustrate beavers and their lodges.

Editorial Credits
Mari C. Schuh, editor; Linda Clavel, series designer; Enoch Peterson, book designer;
     Kelly Garvin, photo researcher; Karen Hieb, product planning editor

Photo Credits
Bruce Coleman Inc./Erwin and Peggy Bauer, 4–5; Jen & Des Bartlett, 15, 21;
     Wolfgang Bayer, 17, 18–19
Corbis/W. Perry Conway, cover
Creatas, 1
North Wind Picture Archives/Nancy Carter, 7
Tom & Pat Leeson, 9, 10–11, 12–13

Note to Parents and Teachers

The Animal Homes series supports national science standards related to life science. This
book describes and illustrates beavers and their lodges. The images support early readers
in understanding the text. The repetition of words and phrases helps early readers learn
new words. This book also introduces early readers to subject-specific vocabulary words,
which are defined in the Glossary section. Early readers may need assistance to read
some words and to use the Table of Contents, Glossary, Read More, Internet Sites, and
Index/Word List sections of the book.

Word Count: 121
Early-Intervention Level: 13

Table of Contents

Building Lodges

Beavers are rodents
that live near water.
Beavers live in lodges.

Beavers build lodges in lakes
and rivers. Beavers work for
days to build their lodges.

Beavers build lodges
with tree branches,
plants, and mud.

Beavers cut down
trees with their teeth.
Beavers gnaw branches
off tree trunks.

Beavers add logs and
branches to the sides
and top of their lodges.

Beavers enter their lodges
through underwater openings.
The openings are hidden
from predators.

Young Beavers

Female beavers give birth
inside lodges. They have
two to four kits at one time.

Kits stay warm and safe inside lodges. Kits stay with their parents for two years.

A Good Home

Adult beavers may live in the same lodge for many years. Lodges are good homes for beavers.

Glossary

gnaw—to bite or chew

kit—a young beaver

lodge—a rounded home made of tree branches, plants, and mud; a family of beavers may work together to build a lodge.

predator—an animal that hunts and eats other animals

rodent—a mammal with large, sharp front teeth for gnawing; beavers, mice, rats, and squirrels are rodents.

Read More

Hall, Margaret. *Beavers.* Wetland Animals. Mankato, Minn.: Pebble Books, 2004.

Jacobs, Lee. *Beaver.* Wild America. San Diego: Blackbirch Press, 2003.

Sullivan, Jody. *Beavers: Big-Toothed Builders.* The Wild World of Animals. Mankato, Minn.: Bridgestone Books, 2003.

Internet Sites

FactHound offers a safe, fun way to find Internet sites related to this book. All of the sites on FactHound have been researched by our staff.

Here's how:

1. Visit *www.facthound.com*

2. Type in this special code **0736825827** for age-appropriate sites. Or enter a search word related to this book for a more general search.

3. Click on the **Fetch It** button.

FactHound will fetch the best sites for you!

Index/Word List